Table of Contents

What is the Stock Market?

The stock market refers to public markets that exist for issuing, buying, and selling stocks that trade on a stock exchange or over-the-counter. Stocks, also known as equities, represent fractional ownership in a company, and the stock market is a place where investors can buy and sell ownership of such investible assets. An efficiently functioning stock market is considered critical to economic development, as it gives companies the ability to quickly access capital from the public.

Purposes of the Stock Market – Capital and Investment Income

The stock market serves two very important purposes. The first is to provide capital to companies that they can use to fund and expand their businesses. If a company issues one million shares of stock that initially sell for $10 a share, then that provides the company with $10 million of capital that it can use to grow its business (minus whatever fees the company pays for an investment bank to manage the stock offering). By offering stock shares instead of borrowing the capital needed for expansion, the company avoids incurring debt and paying interest charges on that debt.

The secondary purpose the stock market serves is to give investors – those who purchase stocks – the opportunity to share in the profits of publicly-traded companies. Investors can profit from stock buying in one of two ways. Some stocks pay regular dividends (a given amount of money per share of stock someone owns). The other way investors can profit from buying stocks is by selling their stock for a profit if the stock price increases from their purchase price. For example, if an investor buys shares of a company's stock at $10 a share and the price of the stock subsequently rises to $15 a share, the investor can then realize a 50% profit on their investment by selling their shares.

How Stocks are Traded – Exchanges and OTC

Most stocks are traded on exchanges such as the New York Stock Exchange (NYSE) or the NASDAQ. Stock exchanges essentially provide the marketplace to facilitate the buying and selling of stocks among investors. Stock exchanges are regulated by government agencies, such as the Securities and Exchange Commission (SEC) in the United States, that oversee the market in order to protect investors from financial fraud and to keep the exchange market functioning smoothly.

Although the vast majority of stocks are traded on exchanges, some stocks are traded over-the-counter (OTC), where buyers and sellers of stocks commonly trade through a dealer, or "market maker", who specifically deals with the stock. OTC stocks are stocks that do not meet the minimum price or other requirements for being listed on exchanges.

OTC stocks are not subject to the same public reporting regulations as stocks listed on exchanges, so it is not as easy for investors to obtain reliable information on the companies issuing such stocks. Stocks in the OTC market are typically much more thinly traded than exchange-traded stocks, which means that investors often must deal with large spreads between bid and ask prices for an OTC stock. In contrast, exchange-traded stocks are much more liquid, with relatively small bid-ask spreads.

Stock Market Players – Investment Banks, Stockbrokers, and Investors

There are a number of regular participants in stock market trading.

Investment banks handle the initial public offering (IPO) of stock that occurs when a company first decides to become a publicly-traded company by offering stock shares.

Here's an example of how an IPO works. A company that wishes to go public and offer shares approaches an investment bank to act as the "underwriter" of the company's initial stock offering. The investment bank, after researching the company's total value and taking into consideration what percentage of ownership the company wishes to relinquish in the form of stock shares, handles the initial issuing of shares in the market in return for a fee, while guaranteeing the company a determined minimum price per share. It is therefore in the best interests of the investment bank to see that all the shares offered are sold and at the highest possible price.

Shares offered in IPOs are most commonly purchased by large institutional investors such as pension funds or mutual fund companies.

The IPO market is known as the primary, or initial, market. Once a stock has been issued in the primary market, all trading in the stock thereafter occurs through the stock exchanges in what is known as the secondary market. The term "secondary market" is a bit misleading, since this is the market where the overwhelming majority of stock trading occurs day to day.

Stockbrokers, who may or may not also be acting as financial advisors, buy and sell stocks for their clients, who may be either institutional investors or individual retail investors.

Equity research analysts may be employed by stock brokerage firms, mutual fund companies, hedge funds, or investment banks. These are individuals who research publicly-traded companies and attempt to forecast whether a company's stock is likely to rise or fall in price.

Fund managers or portfolio managers, which includes hedge fund managers, mutual fund managers, and exchange-traded fund (ETF) managers, are important stock market participants because they buy and sell large quantities of stocks. If a popular mutual fund decides to invest heavily in a particular stock, that demand for the stock alone is often significant enough to drive the stock's price noticeably higher.

Stock Market Indexes

The overall performance of the stock market is usually tracked and reflected in the performance of various stock market indexes. Stock indexes are composed of a selection of stocks that is designed to reflect how stocks are performing overall. Stock market indexes themselves are traded in the form of options and futures contracts, which are also traded on regulated exchanges.

Among the key stock market indexes are the Dow Jones Industrial Average (DJIA), the Standard & Poor's 500 Index (S&P 500), the Financial Times Stock Exchange 100 Index (FTSE 100), the Nikkei 225 Index, the NASDAQ Composite Index, and the Hang Seng Index.

Bull and Bear Markets, and Short Selling

Two of the basic concepts of stock market trading are "bull" and "bear" markets. The term bull market is used to refer to a stock market in which the price of stocks is generally rising. This is the type of market most investors prosper in, as the majority of stock investors are buyers, rather than short-sellers, of stocks. A bear market exists when stock prices are overall declining in price.

Investors can still profit even in bear markets through short selling. Short selling is the practice of borrowing stock that the investor does not hold from a brokerage firm that does own shares of the stock. The investor then sells the borrowed stock shares in the secondary market and receives the money from the sale of that stock. If the stock price declines as the investor hopes, then the investor can realize a profit by purchasing a sufficient number of shares to return to the broker the number of shares they borrowed at a total price less than what they received for selling shares of the stock earlier at a higher price.

For example, if an investor believes that the stock of company "A" is likely to decline from its current price of $20 a share, the investor can put down what is known as a margin deposit in order to borrow 100 shares of the stock from his broker. He then sells those shares for $20 each, the current price, which gives him $2,000. If the stock then falls to $10 a share, the investor can then buy 100 shares to return to his broker for only $1,000, leaving him with a $1,000 profit.

Analyzing Stocks – Market Cap, EPS, and Financial Ratios

Stock market analysts and investors may look at a variety of factors to indicate a stock's probable future direction, up or down in price. Here's a rundown on some of the most commonly viewed variables for stock analysis.

A stock's market capitalization, or market cap, is the total value of all the outstanding shares of the stock. A higher market capitalization usually indicates a company that is more well-established and financially sound.

Publicly traded companies are required by exchange regulatory bodies to regularly provide earnings reports. These reports, issued quarterly and annually, are carefully watched by market analysts as a good indicator of how well a company's business is doing. Among the key factors analyzed from earnings reports are the company's earnings per share (EPS), which reflects the company's profits as divided among all of its outstanding shares of stock.

Analysts and investors also frequently examine a number of financial ratios that are intended to indicate the financial stability, profitability, and growth potential of a publicly-traded company. The following are a few of the key financial ratios that investors and analysts consider:

Price to Earnings (P/E) Ratio: The ratio of a company's stock price in relation to its EPS. A higher P/E ratio indicates that investors are willing to pay higher prices per share for the company's stock because they expect the company to grow and the stock price to rise.

Debt to Equity Ratio: This is a fundamental metric of a company's financial stability, as it shows what percentage of a company's operations are being funded by debt compared to what percentage are being funded by equity investors. A lower debt to equity ratio, indicating primary funding from investors, is preferable.

Return on Equity (ROE) Ratio: The return on equity (ROE) ratio is considered a good indicator of a company's growth potential, as it shows the company's net income relative to the total equity investment in the company.

Profit Margin: There are several profit margin ratios that investors may consider, including operating profit margin and net profit margin. The advantage of looking at profit margin instead of just an absolute dollar profit figure is that it shows what a company's percentage profitability is. For example, a company may show a profit of $2 million, but if that only translates to a 3% profit margin, then any significant decline in revenues may threaten the company's profitability.

Other commonly used financial ratios include return on assets (ROA), dividend yield, price to book (P/B) ratio, current ratio, and the inventory turnover ratio.

Stock Markets around the World

Two Basic Approaches to Stock Market Investing –
Value Investing and Growth Investing

There are countless methods of stock picking that analysts and investors employ, but virtually all of them are one form or another of the two basic stock buying strategies of value investing or growth investing.

Value investors typically invest in well-established companies that have shown steady profitability over a long period of time and may offer regular dividend income. Value investing is more focused on avoiding risk than growth investing is, although value investors do seek to buy stocks when they consider the stock price to be an undervalued bargain.

Growth investors seek out companies with exceptionally high growth potential, hoping to realize maximum appreciation in share price. They are usually less concerned with dividend income and are more willing to risk investing in relatively young companies. Technology stocks, because of their high growth potential, are often favored by growth investors.

What is a Stock?

When a person owns stock in a company, the individual is called a shareholder and is eligible to claim part of the company's residual assets and earnings (should the company ever have to dissolve). A shareholder may also be referred to as a stockholder. The terms "stock", "shares", and "equity" are used interchangeably in modern financial language. The stock market consists of exchanges where investors can buy and sell individual shares of a company.

Most finance career paths will be directly involved with stocks in one way or another, either as an advisor, an issuer, or a buyer.

Benefits of Owning Stocks

There are many potential benefits to owning stocks or shares in a company, including the following:

1. Claim on assets

A shareholder has a claim on assets of a company it has stock in. However, the claims on assets are relevant only when the company faces liquidation. In that event, all of the company's assets and liabilities are counted, and after all creditors are paid, the shareholders can claim what is left. This is the reason that equity (stocks) investments are considered higher risk than debt (credit, loans, and bonds) because creditors are paid before equity holders, and if there are no assets left after the debt is paid, the equity holders may receive nothing.

2. Dividends and Capital Gains

A stockholder may also receive earnings, which are paid in the form of dividends. The company can decide the amount of dividends to be paid in one period (such as one quarter or one year), or it can decide to retain all of the earnings to expand the business further. Aside from dividends, the stockholder can also enjoy capital gains from stock price appreciation.

3. Power to vote

Another powerful feature of stock ownership is that shareholders are entitled to vote for management changes if the company is mismanaged. The executive board of a company will hold annual meetings to report overall company performance. They disclose plans for future period operations and management decisions. Should investors and stockholders disagree with the company's current operation or future plans, they have the power to negotiate changes in management or business strategy.

4. Limited Liability

Lastly, when a person owns shares of a company, the nature of ownership is limited. Should the company go bankrupt, shareholders are not personally liable for any loss.

Risks of Owning Stock

Along with the benefits of stock ownership, there are also risks that investors have to consider, including:

1. Loss of capital

There is no guarantee that a stock's price will move up. An investor may buy shares at $50 during an IPO, but find that the shares move down to $20 as the company begins to perform badly, for example.

2. No liquidation preference

When a company liquidates, creditors are paid before equity holders. In most cases, a company will only liquidate when it has very little assets left to operate. In most cases, that means that there will be no assets left for equity holders once creditors are paid off.

3. Irrelevant power to vote

While retail investors technically have voting rights in executive board meetings, in practice they usually have very limited influence or power. The majority shareholder typically determines the outcome of all votes at shareholder meetings.

Modern Stock Trading

In the past, shares were represented on a piece of paper as a certificate. When a person wanted to purchase shares, they needed to physically visit the office of a broker and make the transaction there, where they would receive the actual share certificates. Today, physical share certificates are rarely seen. Brokers keep documents electronically, and an investor needs only click through online trading platforms to purchase shares.

What Affects Share Prices?

There are many factors that affect share prices. These may include the global economy, sector performance, government policies, natural disasters, and other factors. Investor sentiment – how investors feel about the company's future prospects – often plays a large part in dictating the price. If investors are confident about a company's ability to rapidly grow and eventually produce large returns on investment, then the company's stock price may be well above its current intrinsic, or actual, value.

Two of the most examined financial ratios used to evaluate stocks are the following:

- Revenue growth
- Earnings growth

Revenue growth tells analysts about the sales performance of the company's products or services and generally indicates whether or not its customers love what it does. Earnings reveal how efficiently the company manages its operations and resources to produce profits. Both are very high-level indicators that can be used as references on whether or not to purchase shares. However, stock analysts also use many other financial ratios and tools to help investors profit from equity trading.

No matter what your job in the financial industry, you will be involved with stocks in one way or another.

How do you Calculate Stock Profit

Investors need two numbers to calculate the percentage gain from their stock investments: 1). The original purchase price of the shares, and 2). The price at which the shares were sold at.

Formula For Calculating Stock Profit or Loss

Here is the formula for calculating the percentage move of your stock holdings. Calculating the percentage move will help figure out whether an investor had a good return on investment.

(Price sold – Purchase price)/(Purchase price) X 100% = Percentage move

The important thing about this formula is to always have the purchase price in the denominator. That way the move in the shares is always divided by what an investor paid for them.

Calculating Stock Profit Example

Here's a hypothetical example of using the formula above but incorporating the number of shares an investor may hold. This will give the total dollar profit as well as the percentage move.

1. Let's say an investor owns 100 shares of Stock ABB, which they bought at $20 a share.

2. The investor sells all 100 of their shares when the stock is trading at $23.

3. Ignoring any potential fees, commissions or taxes from this hypothetical example, the investor pockets a tidy profit of $3 per share.

4. Divide $3 by the original purchase price of $20 equals 0.15, which leads to a 15% gain.

Calculating Stock Loss Example

Now let's look at an example where Stock ABB declines.

1. Again, an investor owns 100 shares of Stock ABB, which they bought at $20.

2. But this time, the investor sells all 100 shares at $18.

3. This means, the investor has to subtract $20 from $18 to get negative $2.

4. Dividing negative $2 by the original purchase price of $20 and then multiplying by 100, the loss equals 10%.

Other Income from Stocks

While dividends represent profit from a stock, they are not capital gains.

You may receive income from some stock holdings in the form of dividends, which are unrelated to the sale of the stock. A dividend is a distribution of a portion of a company's profits to a certain class of its shareholders. Dividends may be issued in the form of cash or additional shares of stock.

While dividends represent profit from a stock, they are not capital gains. Dividends can be classified as either qualified or ordinary dividends, which are taxed at different rates. Ordinary dividends are taxed at regular income tax rates.

Qualified dividends that meet certain requirements are subject to the preferential capital gains tax rates. Taxpayers are responsible for identifying the type of dividends they receive and reporting that income on Form 1099-DIV.

Brokerage Fees or Commissions

Then there are brokerage account fees or commissions that you might have paid when you bought the stock. You may have already forgotten about these costs, but they do have an effect on your investment's profitability and depending on their size, could make a profitable trade unprofitable.

You could tally all the fees you paid and subtract that sum from your profit to find out what your net gain was. Note that your brokerage account may do these calculations for you, but you might want to know how to do them yourself to have a better understanding of how the process works.

Before you bust out a pen, paper, and calculator, however, it might be easier to check and see if an online calculator option is available through your broker.

Some brokerage firms offer zero commission trading, but they may be engaging in a practice called payment for order flow, where your orders are sent to third parties in order to be executed.

Capital Gains Taxes

You can subtract the cost basis from total proceeds to calculate what you've made. If the proceeds are greater than the cost basis, you've made a profit, also known as a capital gain. At this point, the government will take a slice of the pie—you'll owe taxes on any capital gains you make.

Capital gains tax rates are the rates at which you're taxed on the profit from selling your stock, in addition to other investments you may hold such as bonds and real estate. You are only taxed on a stock when you sell and realize a gain, and then you are taxed on net gain, which is the difference between gains and losses.

You can deduct capital losses from your gains every year. So if some stocks sell for a profit, while others sell for an equal loss, your net gain could be zero, and you'll owe no taxes on these stocks.

Short-Term vs. Long-Term Capital Gains Taxes

There are two types of capital gains tax that might apply to you: short-term and long-term investment capital gains tax. If you sell a stock you've held for less than a year for a profit, you realize a short-term capital gain.

If you sell a stock you've held for more than a year and profit on the sale, you realize a long-term capital gain. Short-term capital gain tax rates can be significantly higher than long-term rates. These rates are pegged to your tax bracket, and they are taxed as regular income.

So, if your income lands you in the highest tax bracket, you will likely pay a short-term capital gains rate equal to the highest income tax rate— which is quite a bit higher than the highest long-term capital gains rate.

Long-term capital gains, on the other hand, are given preferential tax treatment. Depending on your income and your filing status, you could pay 0%, 15% or a maximum of 20% on gains from investments you've held for more than a year.

Investors may choose to hold on to stocks for a year or more to take advantage of these preferential rates and avoid the higher taxes that may result from the swift buying and selling of stocks inside a year.

When Capital Gains Tax doesn't Apply

There are a few rare instances when you don't have to pay capital gains tax on the profits you make from selling stock, namely inside of retirement accounts.

The government wants you to save for retirement, so they've come up with tax-advantaged investment accounts to encourage you to do so, including 401(k)s and individual retirement accounts.

You fund tax-deferred accounts such as 401(k)s and traditional IRAs with pre-tax dollars, which helps lower your taxable income in the year you make a contribution. You can then buy and sell stocks inside the accounts without incurring any capital gains tax.

These tax-deferred returns can give your savings an extra boost, potentially helping it grow faster than it would in a regular brokerage account. As tax-deferred returns are reinvested, investors are able to take greater advantage of the magic of compounding interest—the returns investors earn on their returns.

Tax-deferred accounts don't allow you to escape taxes entirely however, when you make qualified withdrawals after age 59½, you are taxed at your regular income tax rate. Roth accounts, such as Roth IRAs function slightly differently. You don't escape taxes here either, but you fund these accounts with after-tax dollars.

Then you can then buy and sell stocks inside the account where they can grow tax-free. Once again, you won't owe any capital gains on returns you make inside the account, and when you make withdrawals at age 59½, you won't own any income tax either.

Understanding Capital Losses

Now, let's take a closer look at capital losses. You may be wondering why it would ever make sense to take a capital loss since they are essentially a negative profit. However, capital losses could be an important tool to help you manage your taxes.

Capital losses can be used to offset gains from the sale of other stocks. Say you sold Stock ABB for a profit of $15 and Stock CDD from another company for a loss of $10. The resulting taxable amount is now $5, or $15 minus $10.

In some cases, total losses will be greater than total gains. When this happens, you may be able to deduct excess capital losses against other income.

The amount of losses you can deduct in a given year is limited. However, if you go over this limit, any excess to reduce capital gains in subsequent years could be rolled over into the next year.

There are other limitations with claiming capital losses. The wash sale rule, for example, prohibits claiming a full capital loss after selling securities at a loss and then buying "substantially identical" stocks within a 30-day period.

The rule essentially closes a loophole, preventing investors from selling a stock at a loss only to immediately buy the same security again, leaving their portfolio essentially unchanged while claiming a tax benefit. One way investors try to defer taxes is through automated tax loss harvesting, or strategically taking some losses in order to offset taxable profits from another investment.

When to Consider Selling a Stock

There are a number of reasons investors may choose to sell their stocks and collect a profit. First, they may simply need the money to meet a personal goal, like making a down payment on a home or buying a new car. Investors with retirement accounts may start to liquidate assets in their accounts once they retire and need to make withdrawals.

Stocks that have made significant gains can shift the asset allocation inside an investor's portfolio.

Investors may also choose to sell stocks that have appreciated considerably. Stocks that have made significant gains can shift the asset allocation inside an investor's portfolio. The investor may want to sell stocks and buy other investments to rebalance the portfolio, bringing it back in line with their goals, risk tolerance, and time horizon.

This strategy may give investors the opportunity to sell high and buy low, using appreciated stock to buy new, potentially cheaper, investments. That said, investors might want to avoid trying to time the market, buying and selling based on an attempt to predict future price movements. It's hard to know what the market or any given stock will do in the future.

As a result, timing the market could backfire, leading investors to make expensive mistakes like selling when prices are low and buying as prices are reaching their peak.

Sometimes investors may decide that buying a certain stock was a mistake. It may not be the right match for their goals or risk tolerance, for example. In this case, they may decide to sell it, even if it means incurring a loss.

Advantages of Investing in the Stock Market

Investment Gains

One of the primary benefits of investing in the stock market is the chance to grow your money. Over time, the stock market tends to rise in value, though the prices of individual stocks rise and fall daily. Investments in stable companies that are able to grow tend to make profits for investors. Likewise, investing in many different stocks will help build your wealth by leveraging growth in different sectors of the economy, resulting in a profit even if some of your individual stocks lose value.

Dividend Income

Some stocks provide income in the form of a dividend. While not all stocks offer dividends, those that do deliver annual payments to investors. These payments arrive even if the stock has lost value and represent income on top of any profits that come from eventually selling the stock. Dividend income can help fund a retirement or pay for even more investing as you grow your investment portfolio over time.

Diversification

For investors who put money into different types of investment products, a stock market investment has the benefit of providing diversification. Stock market investments change value independently of other types of investments, such as bonds and real estate. Holding stock can help you weather losses to other investment products. Stock also adds risk to a portfolio, as well as the potential for large, rapid gains, helping investors avoid risk-averse or overly conservative investment strategies.

Ownership

Buying shares of stock means taking on an ownership stake in the company you purchase stock in. This means that investing in the stock market also brings benefits that are part of being one of a business's owners. Shareholders vote on corporate board members and certain business decisions. They also receive annual reports to learn more about the company. Owning stock in the company you work for can be a way to express loyalty and tie your personal finances to the success of the business as a whole.

Stock Calculator (Profit Calculator)

Enter the total number of shares purchased, the purchase price, commission cost, and the selling price, to calculate the total profit and ROI %.

Stock Profit Formula

The following formula can be used to calculate the profit from buying and selling a stock.

$$Profit = [(S * N) - C] - [(P * N) + C]$$

Where S is the selling price of the stock

N is the number of shares sold

C is the %commission taken by the broker for buying and selling

P is the purchase price of the stock

Stock Profit Definition

Stock profit is defined as the total profit earned from the purchase and sale of a stock over some time period.

How to Calculate Stock Profit?

First, determine the purchase price of the stock

Look at the current price of the stock or the past price they were purchased at through your broker.

Next, determine the number of shares purchased

This is as simple as using the number of shares you plan to sell or had bought previously.

Next, determine the % commission taken by the broker

This will typically be the same for purchasing and selling the stock.

Determine the selling price

Check the current price of the stock you plan to sell.

Calculate the stock profit

Enter the information from above into the formula or calculator.

What Is a Stock Market Crash?

A stock market crash is a rapid and often unanticipated drop in stock prices. A stock market crash can be a side effect of a major catastrophic event, economic crisis, or the collapse of a long-term speculative bubble. Reactionary public panic about a stock market crash can also be a major contributor to it, inducing panic selling that depresses prices even further.

Famous stock market crashes include those during the 1929 Great Depression, Black Monday of 1987, the 2001 dotcom bubble burst, the 2008 financial crisis, and during the 2020 COVID-19 pandemic.

Understanding Stock Market Crashes

Although there is no specific threshold for stock market crashes, they are generally considered as abrupt double-digit percentage drop in a stock index over the course of a few days. Stock market crashes often make a significant impact on the economy. Selling shares after a sudden drop in prices and buying too many stocks on margin prior to one are two of the most common ways investors can to lose money when the market crashes.

Well-known U.S. stock market crashes include the market crash of 1929, which resulted from economic decline and panic selling and sparked the Great Depression, and Black Monday (1987), which was also largely caused by investor panic.

Another major crash occurred in 2008 in the housing and real estate market and resulted in what we now refer to as the Great Recession. High-frequency trading was determined to be a cause of the flash crash that occurred in May 2010 and wiped off trillions of dollars from stock prices.

In March 2020, stock markets around the world declined into bear market territory because of the emergence of a pandemic of the COVID-19 coronavirus.

Preventing a Stock Market Crash

Circuit Breakers

Since the crashes of 1929 and 1987, safeguards have been put in place to prevent crashes due to panicked stockholders selling their assets. Such safeguards include trading curbs, or circuit breakers, which prevent any trade activity whatsoever for a certain period of time following a sharp decline in stock prices, in hopes of stabilizing the market and preventing it from falling further.

For example, the New York Stock Exchange (NYSE) has a set of thresholds in place to guard against crashes. They provide for trading halts in all equities and options markets during a severe market decline as measured by a single-day decline in the S&P 500 Index. According to the NYSE:1

A market-wide trading halt can be triggered if the S&P 500 Index declines in price as compared to the prior day's closing price of that index.

The triggers have been set by the markets at three circuit breaker thresholds—7% (Level 1), 13% (Level 2), and 20% (Level 3).

A market decline that triggers a Level 1 or Level 2 circuit breaker after 9:30 a.m. ET and before 3:25 p.m. ET will halt market-wide trading for 15 minutes, while a similar market decline at or after 3:25 p.m. ET will not halt market-wide trading.

A market decline that triggers a Level 3 circuit breaker, at any time during the trading day, will halt market-wide trading for the remainder of the trading day.

Best Stock Market Apps for Android

1. StockTwits

With a powerful combination of social media and stock trading information, StockTwits is one of the most comprehensive android apps. It boasts professionally curated stocklists with real-time data and lots of charts for technical analysis to help traders gauge the market. This app also features a section for forex and cryptocurrencies. Users can also share valuable insights with the community and use the earning calendar to prepare for upcoming events.

Pros

- It features hand-curated stock lists
- Comprehensive crypto and forex section
- Comes with customizable message streams

Cons

- Contains a lot of ads
- You must create an account to use the app

2. Yahoo Finance

Renowned as a top-tier spot for financial information on the internet, Yahoo Finance app is the one-stop-shop for real-time stock market news. This app allows users to track stock price changes, as well as keep an eye on commodities, world markets, equities, and bonds. It also enables you to sync personal stock information across multiple devices.

Pros

- Simple app with a minimalist design and less complicated features
- You can use the app without logging into your yahoo account
- It allows users to create watch lists for real-time stock quotes

Cons

- It features tons of information that is not related to stocks

The combination of cryptocurrencies and commodities make the app somehow confusing

3. Investing.com

Investing.com app boasts all the information that is available on its official website. From live quotes to charts for over 100,000 stocks, this platform has everything you need. It also features financial news for renowned publishers, customizable portfolio screen to track your investment, and customizable alerts.

Pros

- Features a comprehensive list of prominent cryptocurrency prices
- Users can view information about bonds, foreign exchanges, commodities, interest rates, futures and options

- The calendar feature helps traders keep up with finance and business events

Cons

Comes with ads, which are removed at the cost of $1.99 per month

4. Bloomberg

Taking pride in being a trusted name in the financial industry, Bloomberg also powers an android app to help traders monitor global stocks. The app allows you to customize your account and receive just what you want. It also allows users to create their stock portfolio easily.

Pros

- Traders have exclusive access to the Bloomberg live TV
- Boasts a simple and intuitive interface
- Traders can create custom watch lists

Cons

- Comes with loads of information that doesn't relate to the stock market

5. JStock

Integrating a portfolio tracker with a stock market news app, JStock provides you with an easy way to learn about the stock market and track the companies you care about. Simple and efficient, this app delivers the top-notch analysis and places the indices right at your finger trip. It offers customizable snapshots of the entire market.

Pros

- Features tons of information on stock dividends
- Boasts widgets for watch list, portfolio, and world indices
- Simplifies your portfolio in easy-to-understand graphs and charts

Cons

- It doesn't feature the stock trading functionality
- The app requires a one-time $7.99 to start using it

6. Robinhood

Want to buy and track stocks without paying any fees, the Robinhood android app has got you covered. Although it targets beginners, this app provides you with access to charts, historical market data, and financial market organization. Besides, the Robinhood app also permits traders to purchase and sell cryptocurrencies such as Ethereum and Bitcoin.

Pros

- It simplifies the process of buying and selling stocks
- Combining stock and crypto trading is a brilliant idea
- No fees or commissions to start trading

Cons

- The app often crashes on older android devices
- Crypto trading is not available in all the states

7. Stock Quote

Want to get real-time and pre-market quotes and stocks from around the globe at any time of the day, Stock Quote the best app. It features current and insightful business and financial news, as well as relevant posts lifted from social media sites such as Twitter, YouTube, and Facebook. It also gives traders the chance to track and manage their portfolios.

Pros

- The app is available for free
- All the data on the app can be backed up to the cloud via Dropbox, Google Drive or physical SD card
- It offers real-time and pre-market quotes from markets around the world

Cons

- The app could benefit from a design upgrade
- Some users claim that the app is difficult to navigate

8. Real-Time Stocks Tracker

As the name insinuates, Real-time Stocks Tracker is an excellent app that allows users to live stream stock market information. It supports all brokers in the US, and traders can use this app to track multiple watch lists and stock portfolios. It also allows you to customize your search and provides in-depth information about each stock.

Pros

- Provides real-time stocks information
- You can create and watch multiple watch lists and portfolios
- You can set customizable alerts

Cons

- It is littered with loads of unnecessary information.

Best Stock Market Apps in India

1. MoneyControl

Play store rating: 4.1/5 Stars (349k Reviews)

Downloads: +10 Million

Available on: Android, IoS, Windows

This is my personal favorite mobile app for stock market news and updates. If you are planning to keep only one stock market app on your smartphone, then I will highly recommend you to have this one. The money control app is simple, yet has tons of information and news.

You can track the latest updates on Indian and Global financial markets on your smartphone with the Moneycontrol App. It covers multiple assets from BSE, NSE, MCX, and NCDEX exchanges, so you can track Indices (Sensex & Nifty), Stocks, Futures, Options, Mutual Funds, Commodities, and Currencies with ease.

Become A Better Stock Investor

Thousands of stock market investors just like you are using Trade Brains Portal daily to perform a complete fundamental analysis of stocks. Click here to sign up for Trade Brains Portal and start picking winning stocks.

Key Features:

Ease of Use: Easy navigation to all financial data, portfolio, watchlist and message board. Single search bar with voice search for stocks, indices, mutual funds, commodities, news, etc

Latest Market Data: Latest quotes of stocks, F&O, mutual funds, commodities and currencies from BSE, NSE, MCX, and NCDEX

News: All-day coverage of news related to markets, business and economy; plus interviews of senior management

Portfolio: Easy monitoring your portfolio across Stocks, Mutual Funds, ULIPs, and Bullion. Timely updates on the performance of your portfolio, and news & alerts relating to stocks you hold

Personalized Watchlist: Adding your favorite stocks, mutual funds, commodities, futures, and currencies to monitor. Get timely alerts in form of news and corporate action

Message Board: Follow your favorite topics and the top borders to get recommendations. Engage and participate in conversations relating to your portfolio or interest.

2. Stock Edge

Play store rating: 4.4/5 Stars (29k Reviews)

Downloads: +1 Million

Available on: Android, iOS

Stock Edge helps Indian Stock market traders and investors do their own research and make better decisions by providing them with end-of-day analytics and visualizations and alerts.

Key Features

Daily Updates Section for filtered major market tracking with News, NSE & BSE Corporate Announcements, Forthcoming events, & Corporate Actions and more.

FII/ FPI & DII Cash and Derivatives with strong historical data visualization Daily, Monthly & Yearly.

Opportunity Scans: Price Scans, Last week high/ low, Last Month high/ low, 52 weeks high/low, 3 days price behavior, etc

Track what Big Indian Investors are doing. Use MyInvestorGroup section to create your own group of Investors with their multiple names/entities etc

Sector Research: Sector List, Industries in a sector, Companies in a sector/Industry, Price Movement of last 30 days presented in a simple graph, Gainers, Losers etc.

3. Economic Times(ET) Markets

Play store rating: 4.7/5 Stars (45k Stars)

Downloads: +1 Million

Available on: Android, IoS, Windows

This is another of the best stock market apps. I regularly use ET Markets app for reading market news and updates as they provide the best latest news. Moreover, the stock details feature on this app is always very well organized.

Key Features:

To track BSE Sensex, NSE Nifty charts live and get share prices with advanced technical charting.

Follow stock quotes real time, get tips on intraday trading, stock futures, commodities, forex market, ETFs on the go.

One-stop destination for mutual fund news, NAVs, portfolio updates, fund analysis, SIP calculator

Simple swipe to build, manage and access your portfolio; get customized news, analysis and data of the Indian stock market

To create your watchlist and track them regularly

Get analyses/expert views delivered to you, participate in discussions/conversations through comments

4. Tickertape

Play store rating: 4.5/5 Stars (9.3k reviews)

Downloads: +1 Million

Available on: Android, IoS,

This app has become quite popular in the best stock market apps in India in recent months and relatively newer when compared to other apps in this list. Tickertape is a modern stock analysis platform that is designed for keeping you at the center of the process. It focuses on salient metric analysis with powerful tools and robust ecosystem support that can be a catalyst to improve your knowledge about the market and their participation in the same.

Key Features:

Detailed stock analysis for all the publically listed companies in India.

Advanced Screener with 130 filters for you to analyze any Indian stocks.

Market mood Index (MMI) which is the market sentiment indicator trusted to correctly time their trades.

Peer comparisons, news, and events are presented in such a way that will help in your investment decisions.

Finally, Broker Connect to help you log in and connect your broker account to the Tickertape account.

5. Yahoo Finance

Play store rating: 4.1/5 Stars (171k reviews)

Downloads: +10 Million

Available on: Android, IoS, Windows

First of all, after downloading this app, you need to change the settings. In the region settings, select 'India (English)' for getting updates about the Indian stock market. The simple yet dynamic user interface makes it one of the best stock market apps for stock research.

Key Features:

Follow the stocks you care about most and get personalized news and alerts.

Access real-time stock information and investment updates to stay on top of the market.

Add stocks to watchlists to get real-time stock quotes and personalized news

Track the performance of your personal portfolio.

Find all the financial information you need with sleek, intuitive navigation

Go beyond stocks and track currencies, bonds, commodities, equities, world indices, futures, and more

Compare stocks with interactive full-screen charts

6. Market Mojo

Play store rating: 4.2/5 Stars (2k Reviews)

Downloads: +100,000

Available on: Android

This is a new yet powerful app for stock market research. Market Mojo is great for the fundamental analysis of stocks. It offers pre-analyzed information on all stocks, all financials, all news, all price movement, all broker recommendations, all technicals and everything that matters in the Indian stock markets.

Key Features:

The Mojo Quality rank reflects the company's long-term performance vs its peers.

Its Valuation determines how the stock is valued at its current price

The current financial trend indicates if the company is currently on a growth path and its ability to generate profits.

The Portfolio Analyser evaluates every hidden opportunity and risk in the portfolio and tells the investor what he should be doing rather than what he should be just tracking. Every portfolio goes through our test of seven parameters- Returns, Risk, Diversification, Liquidity, Quality, Valuation & Financial Trend

7. Investing.com

Play store rating: 4.6/5 Stars (355k Reviews)

Downloads: +10 Million Downloads

Available on: Android, iOS

Investing.com is a popular stock market app uses worldwide. Along with Indian stock details, you can also find the details about the world indexes and foreign stock exchanges. It offers a set of financial informational tools covering a wide variety of global and local financial instruments.

Key Features:

Live quotes and charts for over 100,000 financial instruments, traded on over 70 global exchanges.

Live updates on global economic events customized to your personal interests.

Build your own customized watchlist and keep track of stock quotes, commodities, indices, ETFs and bonds – all synced with your Investing.com account.

Breaking news, videos, updates and analysis on global financial markets, as well as technology, politics and business.

Quick access to all of our world-class tools, including: Economic Calendar, Earnings Calendar, Technical Summary, Currency Converter, Market Quotes, advanced charts and more.

www.ingramcontent.com/pod-product-compliance
Lightning Source LLC
Chambersburg PA
CBHW062359290526
45794CB00003B/1013